Away with W
A Collection of Poems b

'Away with Words'
A Collection of Poems by Michael Sands

Clachan Publishing
3 Drumavoley Park, Ballycastle, BT54 6PE,
Glens of Antrim.

First published 2014

Email: info@clachanpublishing.com
Website: http://clachanpublishing-com.
ISBN - 978-1-909906-16-7

Clachan Publishing, Ballycastle. The Glens of Antrim.
http://www.clachanpublishing.com

A Collection of Poems

by

Michael Sands

'Away with Words'

For

Catherine, Katie and Tóla

My thoughts are theirs but at the various crossings in our lives, others enter.
I celebrate them all.

Contents

Acknowledgements

We would like to acknowledge and thank the following for the images which appear in this publication:

Cover Painting

- Dónal Ó Dálaigh

Go raibh míle maith agat as an obair den scoth seo a chara mór linn.

Interior pictures –

- Celtic Cross – Pg. 52, Matt Woodhouse
- Dark Hedges – Pg. 12, Kathleen McNeilly
- Swan Park – Pg. 10, Eibhlin Ní Dubhlainn
- Queen's University, Belfast – Pg. 44, Jason O'Rourke
- Thyme & Co., Ballycastle, – Pg. 13, - c/o Thyme & Co Café
- The Piper – Pg. 27, Eoin Jefferies

- All other pictures - Michael Sands

Please support Leukaemia Research.

Foreword

My life has belonged to the black, bitter and twisted trade of journalism, a life of black and white, a world of rights and wrongs, accusations and denials, conflict, division and recriminations.

Then there has been the trade of songwriting. It is a cruel demanding craft bounded by the twin tyrants of rhyme and rhythm. A demanding mistress, it teaches the importance of words, their weight and their value.

What a joy it has been to have discovered this marvellous collection. It represents a bright shaft of welcome sunlight in a wearying world. It is full of joy, hope, intellect and a deep understanding of who we are and the unquestioned importance of hearth, home and music.

To me it is a collection that crosses the T's and dots the I's. It is truthful, thoughtful, touching and tender as well as being intuitive, imaginative, innovative and inspiring.

This poet writes as he speaks and he knows what he is talking about. Read it and enjoy. I cannot recommend it warmly enough.

Mickey MacConnell, Listowel, Co Kerry

May 2014

First Days

It's hard to imagine anything slower than growing up
(especially at the time). The years that define our youth

take an eternity. Or so the leaves in my cup
of memory read. And suddenly an uncomfortable truth,

she's for 'big school' today and he's for primary one.
An unplanned gap to be sure but it has provided

synchronicity, a degree of uniformity for daughter and son.
Our parental twist, strange how their journeys coincided.

She's still our 'wee girl' and forever thus will remain
in spite of any and all achievements beyond

my comprehension. He's our 'big man' who we hope will attain
contentment. A birthday come too soon and gone

denying him time to play for educational captivity.
You worry of course. How will they manage? How will she cope?

How will he be, alone in the classroom? Worried by the gravity
of it all we discuss the future and the past and hope

they'll be OK. But I wouldn't go back. Not a chance.
My school days were red lined and carved 'could do better'

on my mind. The onslaught of a hormonal homework dance,
a subject storm and us subject to the law of the letter.

That was then. New first days have arrived and ushered in-
evitability. We'll grab it and hold on. 'Tis our gift

from the wee ones, which at times we fail to revel in
but will keep us warm when they set themselves adrift.

Twinkle Little Star, Twinkle

Once there was a little star
So far away, oh so very far
And he was sad as sad can be
Down in his melancholy

The light he gave was only half
And it caused his friends to laugh
Nasty names soon he gained
His parents' hearts were sorely pained

A stellar meeting next was held
To see why sorrow in him dwelled
Comets too, meteor showers
The whole affair lasted hours

The senior star to him did ask
"What has taken you to task?
The glow you give is glum and poor
It just won't do of that be sure!"

"Oh what's the point of shining bright?
No one sees me in the night
I do my best but can't compete
With other stars and their white heat."

The senior star sighed indeed
"Listen here and please take heed.
A story yet may change your mind
About a girl of human kind.

Before she went to bed, the sky
In her father's arms caught her eye
Up she looked but only cloud
Was seen, like darkened shroud

Disappointed by the view
A moan was heard from the two
But from the wind a hearty blow
Caused the cloud far to go

A hole therein did appear
What they saw gave them cheer
To sing was all that they could do
For the little star they saw was you!

So always try your best young star
And always wonder what you are
For in this life you never know
Who is gazing from below."

Twinkle twinkle little star
How I wonder what you are…

A Kiss 'til Later

There's a clause in the nine to five, hidden, often missed
that demands the haul from bed at half past seven. This

can be earlier for some, depending on arrangements like
travel, amount of kids, mood of the other half which can spike

and dip and roller coaster. Best to hold the loose thought.
Best not to ask silly questions, for fear of being caught

by the clenched verbal fist of rebuttal or look that asks
"What?!" "Are you serious?!" Best return to one's tasks

which are numerous and queue up rudely and push
each other in the line. A playground offence but in the rush

of it all, a normal state of affairs. Calmness can't tempt
this routine to yield. Such familiarity breeds an unkempt

climate. Change however could melt some glacial features.
Cold shoulders and frosty glares between parents, teachers

of little creatures who see all. They do not much care
for time and boundaries. Long may they inhale the free air.

Not that children are required for early sighs and frantic
searchings for keys, coats, handbags. Hidden by some fairy antic

or other magic for 'they were there last night!' Now nowhere
to be seen. Tick tock. The relentless onward tumble of nature.

And yet there's hope, for comes the moment when the door
opens and fresh thinking enters on a morning breeze. More

than all, a way to keep the world at arm's length,
this moment, between us. A kiss 'til later, for strength.

Decision

For Mum

There is furore in the choice.
An execution of will and the death of a way

to hear not the loudest voice
but discover where truth holds sway.

The consequence of all duly measured
and cast in some negative light,

the positive outcome ought be treasured
not the tempest in the night.

A bridge, a turn a leap o'er faith
I'll look for some guiding hand

Still reverend to our ancient myth
that walked on water o'er sand.

But mine is the moment in which to act.
Deity's silence I choose to hear

and keep my glory all intact
that I would conquer the knave of fear

The burden shouldered and now removed
The id easier having cast the die

No turning back once easily shoved
Coordinated, the mind and eye

Momentum in the lightened road
Excitement in such choices new

Courage gained by courage showed
Contentment knowing what to do

Morning Work

In memory of Pádraig McLean R.I.P

With controlled strain the engine
forces wheels to scatter the mud.
Squelching lost to diesel explosions
belching fumes of earthly erosions
and complain of frost if it could.

The moving earth indignant,
naked without its seasonal costume.
Settling gently in a yellow basket
metal loaded to its waiting casket
worms, slugs and beetles are exhumed.

The distant grounded snore a clue
to pistons, clutch and accelerator.
There is no rest for this machine
e'er the driver's duties to the scene
until tea, bread and biscuits later.

My work demands an explanation
of mechanical groans down on the road.
Sleepy and pyjama'd at the window
peeping at sights there below
Granda smiles with yet another load.

On Rossnowlagh Beach

For Phonsie & Joey

Never quiet, never still
Never sick, never ill

Never empty, never full
Never boring, never dull.

Never anxious, never stressed
Never naked, never dressed

Never crooked, never straight
Never hurried, never late.

Never short, never long
Never right, never wrong

Never humble, never proud
Never calm, never loud.

Never far, never near
Never there, never here

Never white, never black
Never forward, never back.

Never leaves, never stays
Never nights, never days

Rossnowlagh… always

If all was a Breath

For Catherine

If all was a breath, a simple release
Of life having its say

If all that happens did suddenly cease
And this was my last today

If the future itself did now decease
And nothing more pass by this way...

If all was a look, a blink of the eye
In this moment to close

If nothing now came happily by
To see which way the wind blows

If in that glimpse one might indeed try
To undo all those ribbons and bows...

If all was a touch, at our fingertips
The last between you and I

If never again to kiss your cool lips
And feel the heat of your sigh

If now stung sore by life's fillips
Ever wondering, wondering why...

If all was a breath, I'd whisper you
And happily...happily die

Fair Head

Like a great grey leviathan in breach, stilled.
With its eternal edge and ramparts, it greets me.
My journey done and I am full filled
by the deep breath of familiarity.
I revel in the welcome.

It knows I'm here, in its solid embrace,
lost in some ancient affection. About my heart
the want of waves and relief of place
where by rite and magic I am part.
Where now, I am from.

Fair Head, An Bhinn Mhór in earlier refrains.
Its gouged flanks soak me in and release me
tide like, to return and return again
renewed and ready to drift easy
and bob like jetsam.

What intrigue in the secrets of stone,
the non informant of time and age
which sees in me some worth, some unknown
connection. My soul a turning page,
in silence. I am home.

Swan Footprints

For Helen and Roseanne

Five minutes from a door beyond
the normal realm

is our walk. So fairy fond
'neath ash and oak and elm.

Listen. Hear the river rush
over time and ancient stone,

the foaming frothing frantic gush
of water's constant tone.

Dwellings hewn from out the trees,
lights behind the doors,

little ones on bended knees
most curious visitors!

Who can turn themselves to Borrowers
from a library so we

become fleeting followers
of a pen smith or three.

Onward we meander, drawn
to the sea, to stare

briefly into epic tales. The Táin,
the Ulster of what we were

and where magic lives. Clear
to those who choose to see

this distant relative of Lir
who welcomes you and me.

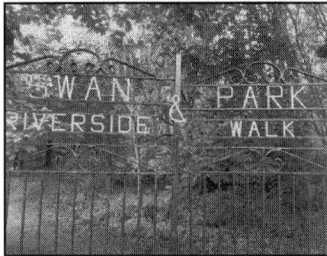

On Ballycastle Beach

My footprints brief across the strand
fall and fade as if some magic hand
bade them disappear.

Our inconsistent friend, the sun,
has returned and so everyone
it seems, has made it here.

The water cool between my toes
caresses me, then off it goes
in its own eternal way.

Ankle deep the sand surround
gives way and I sink on ground
well washed by wave and spray.

Flowered dresses, paler skin
now abundantly exposed. Slowly in-
creasing a rosy hue.

White legged dads, shirts undone
in almost shock, having fun,
can't believe it's true.

Tots and teens, courting pairs
stretch on towels as worldly cares
slip beyond their reach.

And as quick my walk is done
and she is waiting, the one,
for a kiss on Ballycastle beach.

The Dark Hedges

Bound in some ancient mesh the high snakes
of the Hedges await me. That I would dare
walk in their valley? I have unmade mistakes
but not the one to deprive myself of air,

lest I should be denied it by fear. The entangled
symphony of mossy wood high above the soil
regards me lovingly. 'Do come in,' it says, in angled
and vowelled whispers just at the relief of toil.

Even light itself gets scant access, though years
in their thousand number its efforts to radiate
and warm the path below. The Hedges hold no fears
of Sol and but for leaf frailty eternally he'd wait.

So what chance me, a creature of the last second
enjoying beneath? We will find out... Here,
please join me. Take my hand and eye. Be beckoned
by bow and muscular trunk, by twig and near

by craggy bark. By interweaving ivy invaders
who would be our ally. But would they?
Their strangling grasp the tool of raiders
with no love or quality. Their grappling way

would mean the end. Let them fight in slow fury
and us spectate upon it from the dappled road.
In the far tree's shadow a bend. The judge and jury
of their conclusion. Upon its turning all has slowed

and we witness the sun's siege and his failure.
We have survived and are closer to life than before
having chosen such glorious beech exposure.
Fear does not here dwell but magic, myth and lore.

Company and Time

The coffee shop sits near a roundabout. A window
laden with invitation beckons me in. I follow

my nose and invade a table, pushing my chair
and moving a pepper pot. Papered sugars there

both brown and white, make me smile and recall
our young lad eating them, paper and all.

He's at school and will be out soon. The clock
ticks a slow reminder and I'm in shock

at the quiet, the lack of him. I gaze around.
There's a scattering of people, the ground

beans filtering into my senses. Near distant
temptations await me, they know in an instant

I'll break and yield to some soft, sugary fix.
But not yet. Not before real food. More ticks

and several cars roll past. Dulled by glass
to sound almost calming. Outside is chaos.

I turn the waitress away. She smiles and diverts
her path to empty cups and Espresso converts.

Not sipped light brown froth of lattes waits
resolutely at the rim of its empty host as plates

clatter with cutlery. A spray, a wipe, a 'Thanks,
'That was lovely, goodbye'. They return to banks

offices, schools to lick their lips and wish
to stay a little longer. To enjoy another dish

before duty calls. I do not have that burden today.
I am in expectation because she is on her way

with himself. The sugar begins to sweat on hearing
my thoughts. And there they are. Clearing

their space. Hands in the bowl straight away!
We choose not to deter his fingers from play.

My table is complete, not unlike the rhyme
that reminds me to enjoy company and time.

Time of the Month

The waiting is worst. Knowing it's coming.
Until then, anticipation. The delay
that affects mood swings and words can't relay
feelings. Silences and worry becoming

almost too much. Restricted actions
and capped desires in the absence
of certainty. The whim of consequence
hangs over impatient interactions.

Ah what the Hell! We'll risk the wrath
with alacrity to avoid alarm and worry
not over inner arguments to the contrary
for no fury does hot Hell hath

like the scorning of opportunity, of life.
Why else are we here but to explore?
To dare and peer, search and ask for more
than our limits. Be gone cold strife

for it has arrived. We are renewed
by the nature of regularity and can account
better. For therein, by magic, a new amount.
Pay day. And all (for now) is much easier viewed.

New

Culmination, after all. The growing
whisper in the glen. The knowing
looks on a busy street
in town where pairs of feet
face each other and wink and say
'Just hope everything goes ok.'

In conversations. Getting near.
To-ing and fro-ing there and here.
Doctors. Injections. Water
retention. Trials that ought to
be done away with! Closer still.
The midnight flit, the spill

and break of waiting. Anxiety
and a trek of infinite variety
where often none. Traffic fines
defied, to Hell with yellow lines
there's a delivery to be made
into the most caring trade.

And soon… a daughter, a son
one more of us. Another one.
A tiny, fragile piece of you
and me. A future does ensue
with those who can do no more
but love our never here before.

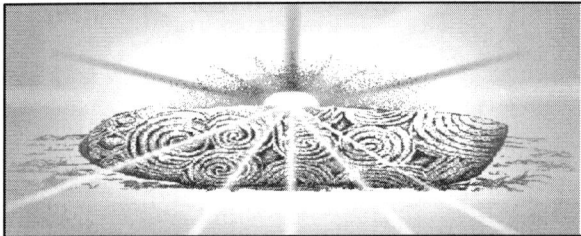

Gift

When we give our child to you
it is **the** most important thing we do.

You hold our beating hearts, our blood,
the little ones that, if possible, we would

never leave. Never miss a single breath
or tear or sigh. Not a one 'til death

takes its cold reward.
To whom of you that we award

our care…Granny, Grandad, teacher, aunt
uncle, friend, sister we simply can't

say thank you loud enough.
Though we may forget with all the stuff

of life, so all you get may be a wave,
it's our souls you tend with love and save.

The Antrim Tantrum

Life's crimson leaves your lips, your eyes adrift and lost
on a sea, dead calm. 'Til tempest wrath reveals the cost

of refusal. A primal wretch against the mother
who now bears more than child birth. No other

sound cuts as deep as anger, your thoughtless rejection.
You deny and throw away as if a sour confection

when all but a moment is required. A brief time alone
to cure the ill. To settle hell, relieve the bile you loan

and scatter gun upon the room. Aimless, you pellet fire
lead expletives, pre sounds. Wordless rage and ire.

Contorted blood twists you, body and mind. Turmoil
at the diverted road. Your plans wrecked and spoiled.

But no one is unduly damaged. For, in spite of all,
the worst of you fades in echo down the hall

and hurts no more. Your fury is afterwards defeated,
spent and realised. It breaks like the completed

splitting of a chestnut and peace is for now restored.
And she is there, holding on. You are still adored

no matter the occasional cantankerous furore.
She understands. She knows. You're only four!

Eleven

For Katie

It is your eleventh year, over half way through
and December's demands for dullness are met.
A coastal mizzle surrounds the town as we do
our best. Wind and cloud weigh heavy and yet

I can see the sun and feel its heat without effort.
Not the great Sol but you, daughter and first
in so many ways. That I would always convert
this to energy or simply admire it or at worst

say thanks. I am guilty at times of being a parent
and not a dad. When stuff of school lies about,
scattered like childish imaginings and the errant
nature of it releases failure in me. I shout

and huff and puff like an old tarmac layer.
Fire and steam and effort to cover all with pitch,
to straighten your road, to say 'I know' like a sayer
of predictions and prophecies. The too tempting itch

of age or at least the want that you avoid mistakes.
But I am not eleven. Mistakes are the celebrations
of youth, of trial and error and they are what make
sense of sense. They are the music and vibrations

of inexperience. I should look more on them so
as you reach the middle of Spring and not far
away I feel a hint of Autumn. Perhaps a hello
or two, a little humility before your sun, your star

will help me pull the horns in, as you might say.
I trust on the silent words we share after the height
of sound. I wrap up warm in the hugs you give each day
and am grateful I can wish you pleasant dreams tonight.

Grass

For Mick and Sue O'Driscoll and boys

I'm with my young lad today. The two of us
men at war, hurling for Cork. "Up the rebels" I shout.
The puck, the catch, the turn, the strike, the rush
of air. Goal! The crowd goes wild. I lift him out

of his standing and we're parading with the best
around Croke park. Well...maybe not exactly.
For we are far from Dublin, farther from the West.
We couldn't be more removed. A fact he

knows little about yet. This is no Baltimore
or Skibbereen or Bantry Bay. This is the land
of exiles. Where every minute by the score
we arrive. And soon have ball and hurl in hand

to remind us of what we are. We'll find a field,
a park, a turn of grass half dead with sun.
But it is real and cold at the root, and will not yield
to cauldrons. It is home, away from everyone.

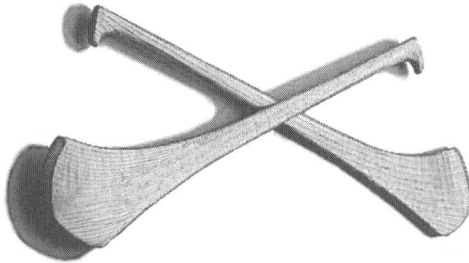

Later

There is something in me. A wont
to forget the time, the date, the message.

To not write the list. So I don't
organise or keep ideas on a page.

It does not lead to an easier time.
If anything a certain chaos reigns

as I begin the assault, the climb
up and round the brambled lanes

of inquiry. The wheres and whens.
The shock of forgotten agreements

not recorded in the memory of pens
or pencils. No, that would make sense.

That would be to conform, to submit,
to yield. To what? The promise of 'yes'?

To follow up with purpose and commit
to actually doing, responding. No less.

No more, for there is rebellion in me.
One's personal war against rules

and regulations. I'll deny and be free
of laws learned in offices and schools.

Opinionated

It would seem all I have are opinions.
Reflexing mind muscles in need of measure
built in and plough-pathed to grow at their leisure,
mocking civility and all of her minions

whose contempt is an eyelid's flutter
a downward look, an eyebrow ascending.
Loyal to fear and correctness unbending,
not what is caught in one's own whirring shutter.

To forego the chaff of the more trodden road
and vanquish humility's dragon.
To drink honesty's wrath by the flagon
and shelve the mind's wearisome load

would appear the brave choice to make,
many would say the right thing to do.
But the troublesome direct point of view
makes its selection feel a mistake.

The inner, the id, the interior I.D.
where most of me sits pure and alone.
The outer enters this intricate zone
to create some fleeting personality.

This delicate often teetering role
played out in battle fatigues.
Unearthing argument, diversion, intrigues
and plots representing the soul.

Ode to Bitterness

If not for anger then what would I crave?
To keep me alive. To know what I hate.
If that bastard I went and forgave
refused my hand twisted by fate. What then?

Everyone must know what happened to me.
How could I turn the other cheek
and turn the dead with such sympathy?
The disgruntled, me, surely would seek.

The pain is too much to ever let go
wrapped as I am in its charmless hue.
And by yielding would the world know
What was done to me, and done to you?

How in God's name could I ever forget
what they did. Them and their kind?
No, bitterness will keep me sweet a while yet
just the thing for an ill tempered mind.

You think it's fun? This chilled certainty?
Work is required, to keep the heart cold.
Come here, I don't want to be free
of this curable frost, truth be told.

And what if my eyes hide under a frown?
So what if my face is wrinkled and sore?
I stood up for anger and didn't back down
like God and the Divil I've got plenty more.

Do you think frustration is easy ignored?
There on my shoulders all heavy and proud
walking beside me in thoughts over pored
and in my words now spoken aloud.

Leave it behind? Give my head peace?
Would that I could? No, probably not.
What did Jesus do with Rome at his knees?
He died. Died for me? Died for what?

No Glory in War

A rat is eating my brother's left eye. It is not thin
or scrawny and clings to life, unlike my brother.

He is bent over at wrong angles and his pallid skin
denies hope. The air is rancid around us. Other

smells include vomit, shit and piss. The gas
mask is some relief although I threw up in it

yesterday. That was his last day. He fell as
we laughed about a cow at home. I lit

a match and held it to his cigarette.
He inhaled the tobacco and drew no further breath

as it was taken by the push of a bayonet
through his stomach and on to death.

Today, I am crammed into water and mud,
ankle deep. I don't feel my feet. The feet

that walked excitedly with his. If I could
retrace them now I'd choose a different street.

Not the one with the posters and Royal approval
of fighting for freedom in this great war

of cousins. The cause of our uniformed removal
from home, loved ones and all that we are.

Now we are no more than a reason for rifle
salutes and bugles. No more than a lesson to learn

in futility. My eyes are scorched so that we stifle
an empire and build another as thousands burn.

My fellows lie about me, shell shocked, half dead,
half mad. They babble of Coventry and Leeds.

Some call for their mothers. They squeal as the lead
crosses flesh borders and are far from daring deeds.

I shall not inter my brother. He is fodder for vermin
and flies. His stench betrays the life our mother gave.

To die like this after her efforts. Religion has no sermon
to redeem the likes of me. I have found my grave.

Hurt

It's not like hurt just goes away
to bathe in angst or regret
or shall we say
remorse.
No, it hangs around. It lingers
until perhaps understanding is its foil
and does likewise toil
through need and kneading fingers.

Funeral Exit

To stand and listen as indeed one must
to the reluctant tea laden throng,
would seem a study in the human dust
that shall reclaim us all before long.

Compliments, tall as the fresh cut bread
that passes from plate to plate in small talk
soon droop, as far from the coffin bed
the true nature of feelings stalk.

"Between you and me… (here it comes)
He was a '(suitable rural expletive'!)"
In safe company these acid crumbs
are shared by the wary collective.

"Ach there's the wife, God love 'er,"
They say, then spit hard on tar
and cough up phlegm in mid prayer
mouth mumbled en route to the car.

Upon the grass verge black polish and green
meet briefly, as long coats fail
to avoid the hedge and shoes too clean
squeeze bunions and an in growing toe nail.

Relief comes in the rough of the pub
where recantations of him sit well
with whisky, and the general hubbub
of the half truths about money they tell.

The Pipes

(for Patrick O'Hare)

It begins at the elbow. And with straps all tightened
he'll fill the bag. Deep draws of breath like frightened

gasps until the pressure is just so. Almost there.
But the tapping must follow. Tuning the air

trapped in drones, regulators and chanter.
It rushes out in mixed pitches, unique reedy banter,

the sound of ages. At last the time has come.
The air store squeezed as if persuading some

delicate terror. The bellows swiftly supply
wind suddenly released over the reed to fly

gloriously. Oh what sound. The rasp, cut and squeal
of freedom itself. But it must come to heal.

Quickly his fingers steer and clear the path
of familiar breezes wrapped in fire and wrath.

Still he pumps and the lower elements are heard
like an earthen growl. All working together

defying the world, captivity and restrain.
The pipes...how I long to hear them once again.

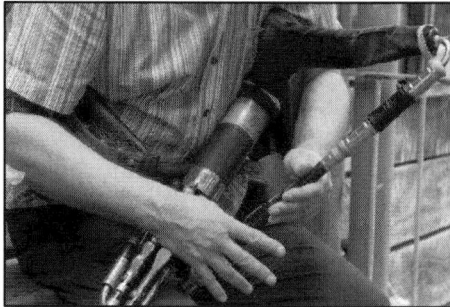

In Session

(for Ireland's traditional musicians and singers)

The tune turns. The shout, the call.
Rolling waves crash upon rocks

as fingers on notes crescendo. All
defining the tick of traditional clocks.

Timepieces we that search out the key
of comparison, reassurance and tone.

The endless pursuit of melody
and harmonies that are never alone

in the circle. The table, the drink,
the tuning, the seats, the cases,

the minim of magic. The clink
of glasses and smiles on faces

that don't often meet nowadays.
Infrequent but welcome, no bother.

"Sit down and play," she says.
"We'll find you one way or another."

And into it. Freedom, from fears,
to play like the devil was waiting.

He can wait fifty damned years
we live! For this. Undulating

and twisting. Rising and still
reaching higher than sight

can impede. Through walls until
a break. A pause in the night.

But only that. A brief inhalation
to rosin the bow, retune a peg,

refill the glass, deny dehydration,
stretch out the fingers, shake a leg

and into it. Again. For as long
as the ear can see. Our choice

of liberty through music and song
and tradition. This is our voice.

Corner Man

For Maurice Lennon

We came in out of the night a little overdressed
for the session. We'd had dinner with new faces.

This was dessert and we could not have guessed
on its quality. The low ceiling felt good, places

in Ireland are full of them but we were far removed.
The music though was a warm greeting

and we stayed in the shadows, listening to loved
tunes and versions. What chance the meeting

with himself? For there he was on a small stage,
dimly lit with the merest hint of attention.

But he cared little. I stared as echoes of an earlier age
nudged my ribs. 'It's him!' I hardly dared mention

his name. In front of us, live! Not carried via cd
or recording but there not ten yards away.

Our common language was the jig and the reel
and he bade us join. 'Honoured' was all I could say.

He talked of settings, fleadhs and mighty tunes
learned from uncles and other aged sources.

We listened like children do when for those few
summers awe runs through us and forces

us to wonder. He confided that life had been hard
of late, information neither of us had earned.

But in the youth of acquaintance truth is unmarred
and something shared is something learned.

We understood and he began again on the high E
a slow air that next door's loud and empty din

could not deflate. His bow whispered calmly to me
and I caught her eye, 'twas royal company we were in.

The heat off such players scalds many unassuming
corners and burned memories wait in the walls.

We go to seek them out, on the all consuming
journey that traditional music calls.

Amnesia

That special island, I heard them say,
saints and scholars, little people.
Various types of sky borne steeple
where chastened knees bend to pray.

Music and sport would seem the norm
and betting rich for gamblers.
A mountained land for ramblers
where the whiskey keeps you warm.

But lesser now. The more we wanted
Fast money. As quickly gone
to other banks to lend and lean on.
Debt has left us less enchanted.

To return in haste the borrowed thing,
the lender's conscience to relieve.
This shackled country now must grieve
and mourn the empty dreams we bring.

Were we not the Emerald Isle?
That sea green diamond all aglow?
Whose lustre now is far below
the sparkle of a loving smile.

For greed became our bosom pal
and having slapped our backs with loot
now kicks away the harp and flute,
we shudder in this petit mal.

Our language pecked by modern crows,
our music deafened in the night,
our writing hidden out of sight
by an upward turning of the nose.

Ireland you were my most beloved
but a stranger now I only see.
Having turned your back on me
wealth it seems is what you covet.

Why does shame now cloud your eyes?
You bow before the pound of flesh
and deny this self deluding mesh
of affluence in some poor disguise.

From May so bright to dark September
your shoulders hunched against the cold,
my Kathleen now so weak and old
Who are you? I can't remember.

Uluru

For Troy Allen

I hear Troy's words in my head, now that we're here.
Here at the heart of it, the red stone heart of Australia.

I see him and his mob dancing, kicking up dirt, spear
waving, catching fish in dreamtime. Utopia?

Yes. For us. Visitors. Short term residents from afar.
Too far to see the black and white of it, colour blind

but sympathetic. We relate and share some similar scars.
At least I think we do, we Irish. Warm and kind,

fond of a tune. But I fear we do not understand Troy.
His ancient ghost mocks my suit, my cuffs and tie,

the garb of western white fellas. He cares not for corduroy
or straightness. His clothes are unruly, unbound and do not shy

from nature. They cover him and reveal his soul
for those who care to see it. Not much glitters in shacks

and reservations save for perhaps sunlit beer on dole
mornings. Or the doctor's pen after diabetes attacks.

The other Australia that we do not visit makes its request
'Look at me. Listen to me' it says. 'What do you see?'

Through every empty tin, worn shoe and too tight vest,
I conclude it not befitting of such dignified antiquity.

The grass at Uluru is harsh and to the point but survives
all onslaughts. Our walk around it swelters our pink skin.

Similar skin is found in capitals and nonchalantly thrives
on many apathies. Ask them just who's country are we in?

Walkers

I live amid a benign conflict. Or so it feels.
The old town of the castle accommodates two clans,

infinitely varied and each unique in how their heels
hit the ground. Different in outlook, manner and plans.

With the low sun of November, Anne Street raises your hand.
I cover my eyes and see him approach, with dirt

on him but not dirty. He squints too after a soiled and
familiar potato tractor, a Fergie. He turns, his shirt

in uproar against his stomach. A blazer clashes with tilled
mud on capped working boots and his determination.

I side step just as he marches passed. Strong willed,
and will not be stopping, though he offers salutation.

I stare after him a moment to think something and see
a different fellow entirely who has perhaps never worn a cap

or Wellingtons. He ascends Castle Street into winter. He's
a lawyer maybe? Chemist? An interior man on another lap

of the nine to five hundred. No such insurgence
from his elegant attire, his socks are silent and well heeled.

The ice blue of his top half creates no divergence
with the far from threadbare bottom, an area needle sealed

and padded to perfection. Away to their work the pair
to make their errands count, whatever they may be.

The Diamond welcomes many walkers, here and there,
unaware it seems their steps make for poetry.

Quay Road Labourers

Such men do not use a brush
to sweep the kitchen floor. Nor do they rush
behind the door to hang a coat upon a hook.
In the home are they not inclined
to do all they're asked. They'd rather be reclined
than to be tasked with little jobs they overlook.

Today I saw them stand together
layer wrapped in boots against the weather,
their working suits, the uniform of rough and ready.
The winter wind did heartless blow
as escaped their breath against this bitter foe
that felt like death observing, calm and steady.

I bade them greeting as I passed
and humbled by their smiles and all steadfast
I hoped such trials behind wherever more I went.
I thought perhaps I would not choose
this manner of accrual. What courage must enthuse
through those gruel clouds before a day is spent.

For there against the edge of cold
they tidied. They swept the brush, as a voice not old
their wishes kept in the hours that wile away.
Pride and will are forced to wait
on another opportunity. These men obey or negate
with impunity whatever profit made that day.

I ask myself has fortune shone
on me that no more does rise before the dawn
to labour's chore and scattering of my soul?
Or by not grafting in this way
am I unequal? My warm and convoluted day
has no sequel that can match the digging of a hole.

On Meeting an Old School Teacher

I don't believe it, I thought, seeing him there,
in the doorway, no change on him. Well, less hair

than during school days, days of fragmentation.
We exchanged names, assuaging quickly the occasion

that marked him present. 'Just work stuff,' he smiled,
recomposed. No longer my teacher, just a man, piled

into an appointment with a stranger to both of us.
We travelled twenty years in one minute, without fuss

or formality. The commonality of our early district
our bond and much stronger than any slightly strict

lesson he oversaw. We did not lock horns or engage
much in lessons and I held no memory of rage.

Indeed, I was happy to see him for he carried more
than he knew. From his classroom store

of recall we discussed old neighbours and echoes
of their lives. I knew nearly all and each proposed

the notion of being removed. 'You're up here now?'
'Yes, married with two and a little more know how

than yesterday.' He fulfilled his engagement
and returned, allowing for our estrangement

to be ended. He gave me a little of his story
and a sadness accompanied him but not before

he shook my hand. 'It's a small world indeed.
A Saval man, far from home and the Irish Sea

a neighbour.' I acknowledged his grip
and gave it back. 'If you do ever make the trip

back, give me a shout.' We exchanged contact
details and he was gone, as if something inexact

had happened. A new lesson and an old rule,
not to gauge too much by what went on at school.

A Natural Hi

for Tóla

There is a softness in grassy ground that soothes my bones.
The compromise of soil, the ligaments of earth and sky.

Each step thereon is a massage of sorts. No phones
or web except for woven web cots ankle high.

A retreat for some buzzing thing that will swoop me on walks.
Or more likely I'll flail at it with my humanity,

whatever that is. I am the stranger to nature that stalks
the middle world of achievement, finance and vanity.

I do wish it different. I would have beer with blackthorns,
sup nectar with bees and discuss stones with lichen or moss.

I would listen to crows talk about architecture, all secret sworn.
I could advise them on colour for it seems they are at a loss

with regard to it. A rabbit or fox could tell me of fear.
A cow or a sheep could explain the uncomfortable truth

of potential unfulfilled. The white bull may be keen to hear
my thoughts on the sex industry. I could quench any druth

or drought of knowledge in the stream sadly too clear
of fish shadows or frogs. I have not been circumspect

with the stuff I throw away and turn away from for fear
I'll have to turn back and treat it, with respect.

My every thread a plastic and contaminant, from head to toe.
From gumboot to oil coat to confection cover discarded

and strewn lifeless and longing. Perhaps, I should merely go
and offer this ground some of me, my soul open and unguarded,

and say hello. I could listen the way a daughter or a son would
to this most unique parent, who affects me like a mother

but will now scold because continually I do what I should
not. It is in her paradise I'll find my way, there is no other.

Culfeightrin Chapel from its Gate

Yellow clumps of pointedness enveloping a hill.
The future of us all
still, and growing.

Walled and mossy stones exhibiting the skill
of Heaven's selective reach
and knowing.

Exiled to a cornered patch eager grass will sway
before its holy duty
and sorrow flowing.

The rest long departed beneath the blessed clay
from excruciating wombs
to mark them going.

Delicate disturbing steepness, the families' coloured plots
captured in a frame
from cots, congregating.

To the fruitful lives with time at beauty spots
and now depart
from us, separating.

Omnipotent the building, central to the theme
triangled turrets point
straight ahead, debating.

Tar and trees aligning life's eternal scheme
that makes us stand
alone, and waiting.

The Last Favour

They approach in silence knowing their work. The plot
has lain easy for years. His neighbours arrange turns,

well ordered. The company marks a death but not
of just anyone, Carey mourns as it learns

of his passing. Contact had been swift, they ready for toil.
The engine growls as quietly as it can on holy ground

and pierces the earth drawing out fresh brown soil
along with those ornamental stones found

at graves to decorate silence. The headstones beyond
stand and wait. They watch as the mound grows higher.

This most noble of favours , yet undesired, so fond
and true is his memory. But none deny him nor tire

'til the planks are brought across and the shovels rest.
In a short while all is prepared and as well crafted

as can be. A few words break the wind's stern test
and chill. 'That's it lads.' Nothing else after.

The parish gathers itself for the repose of his soul.
It will stand quietly by these efforts in a day or two

as will his family, friends and those that dug the hole.
Those that are close know what friends will do.

Finn - A Dubliner in the Glens

For Finn, a good dog

He didn't say much at all. It was only on the rare occasion
you'd get anything out of him, an utterance from the deep.

Surprising for a Dubliner, not ones for evasion
of opinions those boys (famous for wit and can keep

any party afloat). In his youth he was quiet, almost shy,
but playful, cheeky too. A constant interruption for older folks,

Flo, in particular. We wondered if perhaps an extra eye
would help her anticipation. She was often the brunt of jokes

and japes in general. Her years brought little protection
or respect. Conversations ended with her back turned,

which eventually guided his energies in the right direction.
Then beckoned a new home and new lessons to be learned

up north, in the glens. He left Newry without complaint,
compliant as ever. We asked how he was but no sound,

save for a look. Temptations of the flesh proved him no saint
at times. We worried if his exploits would get around.

People do love to talk but if concerned, he never said.
There were many moonlit moves to secret destinations

but we forgave him (though he never asked) and played
the innocent with ease after such lusty peregrinations!

He fitted in you see. To the glens, the scenery, to us
and was family though not by blood. More than blood, he was

a comment on us all. As the years accrued he adapted without fuss
to children and neighbour's children, kindness is as kindness does.

Until all of a sudden he was slow and weak, unfit and afraid
and just not himself. As caring but unable to do as before

and spent the day in slumber as if the end had been delayed
for something. He never told and as soon was no more.

No less in our hearts. No less the warmth of recollection
of this true companion. At rest now in Antrim

amongst those who have left memories for our selection
and those that will ever think fondly of him.

Night Visit

for Tóla

People say it's rude to stare, but really I do not care
at least not here.
You came to us last night half sleeping, for safe keeping
from your fear.

We lit the lamp and made a space, a magic place
all warm and sure.
In between your mum and dad, good dreams were had
and nightmares cured.

You said the trees were much too loud, and the clouds
were sharp and sore
or so I think I heard you say. But happily far from day
you began to snore.

And now we wake with our plus one, our pj'd son
near upside down.
Rolling that way and this, you deny a morning kiss
until turned around.

Your feet somewhere near my nose, slumbering atop bed clothes
pillows all asunder.
Your mum adjusts your head and feet, soon again beneath the sheet
leaving me to wonder

at such moments red and rosy, the world away and us as cosy
as love is near.
People say it's rude to stare, but really I do not care
at least not here.

Whale Winged

for Francis O'Hare

Swallows or swifts? No, definitely not
but swallowing swift on special brewed gut rot

we were the Walrus Two or is that Walrii?
(Walruses apparently) Which covers well you and I.

Up University Street we sideways meandered
('Cos we sure as shite sticks didn't do dandered).

'Lamped' in drunk speak, yes that's the one,
the spilling of all things under the sun

from long now abandoned stomachs and minds.
And would explain why we were on our behinds

in amongst Queen's resilient shrubbery
our legs camouflaged, like stems all rubbery.

No net required, there was no trapeze.
We spurned the safe path while shooting the breeze.

Heads rented room to a new tenant lump.
Well, there *was* a wall, so we both *had* to jump.

Perhaps in the air for a second, not sure,
but what a start to a horticultural tour

of close up green leaves and pointy out roots,
old Beatle tracks, good weed and oul' boots.

But the end was just small change for the means
on a slow walk home that night up past Queen's.

Three yards gapped the two footed abyss
mountain goated in our Dutch-couraged assuredness.

"Once more unto the beech!" Or the birch
was the eager call en route to the lurch

into oblivion. But we *had* conquered the wall
like caped crusaders, though not super at all.

We flew like cluster bombs scattering jeans
and elbow leather to the deep evergreens

on a slow walk home that night up past Queen's,
in Protestant red bricks, lit up for the teens

whom it would entice with promises rich.
Which seemed on us lost at that time in the ditch.

Then we stood up and as quickly were gone
to some other adventure to share memories on.

But what do you *really* do?

It is often with dread I answer that question,
the one that asks me, "What do you do?"

For words and music don't offer suggestion
at describing their uses in society's view.

Yes, there is 'writer' and 'musician' no doubt
but do they convey any more than the word?

Do they explain what they are about
without sounding aloof or a little absurd?

For when they are uttered, faces look back
with respect to be sure but also with guile

that bodes a sort of well mannered attack
beginning with a rather dubious smile.

"But what do you *really* do, other than that?
What is the work upon which you toil?

Your bread and butter, the grind, all that?
Real work that pays, like digging in soil

or building a house, or cooking the books
or an effort at least that might make you sweat."

I'll yield to assuage disparaging looks
with my attempts to ensure ends are best met

and say, 'Clerk, waiter, bar man, assistant,
attendant, porter, sales rep or other.'

Different ways to appease the persistent
need to provide for oneself or another.

For there is no profit in my life's pursuit
of tumultuous tunes or fabulous phrases,

days spent dreaming and not in a suit,
hours spent listening, lost in word mazes.

Except that there is. *Really*. All unseen
by eyes that can not see beyond reason.

It is pure gold, eternity, all ever green,
Shangri La, the change of the season

and is why I, we, do it. We are the hunters,
the gatherers of art and expressions,

the inner sanctuary for life weary punters
to hear, see and touch such souls' confessions.

Where are ye from?

She asked in a breath, 'Where are ye from?
I made to reply but was quickly struck dumb.

For I expanded her question, (the possibility
of more than one answer a high probability).

I stared at her eyes, her warm smiling face
and asked, 'You mean now? Or should I retrace

to former abodes for I am not from here.
Though 'tis here I now live. Am I being clear?'

She sipped on her wine in a manner that said,
'Elaborate (if you must) lest such be delayed.'

'Quickly,' thought I. 'Let there be little fuss.'
Not knowing where her question would take us.

'I began life in London though I am not from there.
I'm no Cockney rebel and for it don't care.

No offence. 'None taken.' I left very young
Just a babe in fact when the changes were rung.

'Where was it next?' she asked as she tasted
more fruit of the vine and not a drop wasted.

'Lurgan' said I. 'I spent there nine years.
Some ups and downs of course, laughter and tears.'

'So, you're from Armagh?' Her innocent conclusion.
Said I, 'Not a hope!' to increase her confusion.

From there it was Newry to which I did venture
and seventeen tours of the sun's great adventure

I had in that town. It still calls me back
but I shall not return to my dear red and black.'

Her eyebrows shot up, then fell to a frown
'But Armagh is one half, the other is Down.

So in Down you resided while in that town?'
'Sadly no,' said I. 'Fate me messed around.'

'I'm Down to the core but alas you speak true.
Exiled in Armagh, not a thing I could do.'

Her glass quickly empty she ordered again
(Curiosity's thirst) I would have to explain.

My kin are from Down and still there enjoy
the mountains and streams where I roamed a boy.

'Uh huh,' she offered, then asked sharp and clear,
'How in God's name did you get to be here?'

'Love brought me north to live 'til I perish
With a gorgeous wee girl 'tis her I most cherish.'

A Ballycastle girl ye decided to marry?'
'Well no, not exactly, she hails from Carey.'

'Oh God I give up! Tom, serve me a rum.
And remind me never ask a man where's he from!'

Bad Blood

We are bound, though we may not know
how many. We know our numbers swell

daily in a frightening and chilling flow
of reports and statistics. They coldly tell

of its grasp. A grasp that rarely releases
those once held. Except to die and leave

such sorrow behind that never ceases.
Yet some of us remain. Hard to believe

I am one. And of the other
I can say he is thankful to be here.

In this illness, this bad blood, we are brother
and comrade. Warriors against fear

and hopelessness. For in recovery
we see. We have a little insight

into difference. This difficult discovery
frustrates notions of winning. Of right

and wrong, Orange and Green,
eclipsed as they are by life itself.

Sunspots on the face of a serene
light. We'll set them aside on a shelf.

We who now have received the gift
of survival. Why conquer cancer

if only to retrace war paths and lift
more bad blood? I see no answer.

Makes Perfect

It then disappears, like lighthouse light,
leaving me at odds, lost, all at sea.
But some thing drives me on. The sight
of it, the flash awakens determination in me.

I pull back the oars of my discipline,
a time goes by without want of measure.
I repeat and fail 'til patience wears thin.
Another beam, as if guiding to treasure,

forces me deeper and battle is met.
I fear the tide will drown my endeavour
and I bob in long moments. Oh, me beset
with improvement! But wishing never

gained a yard of ground. I re-bury fatigue.
I doubt my eyes but it soon re-appears,
not beyond the outline of land, a league
away. Not too far, not as far as my fears.

Dawn. It's promise creeps into me
enough that I raise my head to the call
of other boatmen and women. This company
of sailors, I greet each one and all.

Through such journeys small and unique
our destination is shared in that distance.
In meetings, of what tales we will speak
we who see the worth of persistence.

Who was I?

I am but puddle deep, the skip of a stone.
Yet I crave deep places; the caverns and tombs

of my predecessors. They strode before and own
my curiosity, my respect. From such wombs

came I, hungry for contact, for some link
to justify my passions. To make sense of queries

regarding identity, kinship. How should I think
on the past and present? Such a mixture of theories

and practices. A process of ideas and ways
that has me here and now asking, wondering,

who was I? Why am I spending days
searching? Was I a raider? A knave? Plundering

treasures? Did I fight them blade in hand?
Did marriage grant me join them? Oh to know.

What sound my tongue? Did I shout and stand
defiant and curse them in some ebb and flow

of vowels and consonants that was not theirs?
Did I worship the sun, the rivers, the trees

or did a new God save me? Many say prayers
still, not in standing, they do so on their knees.

A learned behaviour, civilised some would claim
to bow and doff ones' cap to those that wave

from balconies and see little more than shame
in poverty and struggle. 'Tis easy to be brave

far from the front line, the picket line or bread line.
My influences lean me away from aristocracy.

I have no desire to lean back or myself entwine
in it. I prefer the artistic democracy

of music, literature, craft and learning
from those ancient echoes, resounding still.

Each one evokes some mystery, a yearning
to appreciate their workings and I will

not abandon them. To do so is to turn
away and I am not fool enough to deny

such raptures, such devices wherein I may learn
who I was and with patience...who am I.

Re-Unification

The separation was forced,
with little, if any, choice.

A little history off course
and that smaller voice

ignored, for the greater good?
The powers that be

left much misunderstood.
Oh, to be free

of it. To run and shout
without the oppression

of overseers. To flout
laws without confession.

But no, we are restricted
in thought and deed.

And are conflicted
as we remain un-freed.

The punishment was steep
although lesser now.

But memories of pain keep
the echoes aloud,

lest we forget injustice.
My comrades as one

used to the practice
of celebrating each day done.

For at the very end
we see the promise

of completion and depend
on that loving kiss

to keep going, to compel
ourselves. Victory is had

when I hear the bell...
and hug my mum and dad.

Just Checking…just in case

The last turn before sleep is your room.
Curiosity and compassion draw me in
to check. Just to see. To allay the ides of doom
that whisper, mumble, roar and scream within.

Silence. Oh God! No wait! A half lit sigh
deep, from a corner of the bed.
I edge along avoiding the dinosaurs that lie
in strange places with trains blue and red.

I dare not breathe for fear you'll wake.
I bend. A closer look at your well shut eyes
reveals beauty. Perfection. I stare and take
you in. At peace, in dreams with dragon flies.

Satisfied. I retrace my careful path
but you stir! A gargled word. Expletives I resist
and save them for those in need of wrath.
Calmer, your forehead to have kissed

Clachan's 'Historic Irish Journeys' series

Travels In Ireland - J.G. Kohl

This is a very readable account by a German visitor of his tour around Ireland immediately before the Great Famine.

Disturbed Ireland – 1881 - Bernard Becker

A series of letters written as the author travelled around the West of Ireland, visiting key places in the 'Land War'. We meet Captain Boycott and other members of the gentry, as well as a range of small farmers and peasants.

A Journey throughout Ireland, During the Spring, Summer and Autumn of 1834 - Henry D. Inglis

Inglis travels Ireland attempting to answer the question, 'is Ireland and improving country?' using discussion with landlords, manufacturers and tenants plus his own insightful observations.

The West Of Ireland: Its Existing Condition and Prospects - Henry Coulter

This is a collection of letters from *Saunders's News-Letter* relating to the condition and prospects of the people of the West of Ireland after the partial failure of the harvests of the early 1860s.

Highways and Byways in Donegal and Antrim - Stephen Gwynn

If you take this wonderful account of a bike journey written at the end of the 19th Century with you as you travel around Donegal and the Glens of Antrim and you will journey not only over land, but also over time.

*   *   *   *   *

Clachan 'Local History' Series

Henry Coulter's account has been sub-divided for the convenience of local and family historians.

The West Of Ireland: Its Existing Condition and Prospects, Part 1, by Henry Coulter. This is an extract from the complete edition dealing with Athlone, Co. Clare and Co. Galway.

The West Of Ireland: Its Existing Condition and Prospects, Part 2, by Henry Coulter. This is an extract from the complete edition dealing with Co. Mayo.

The West Of Ireland: Its Existing Condition and Prospects, Part 3, by Henry Coulter. The final extract from the complete edition dealing with Counties Co Sligo, Donegal, Leitrim and Roscommon.

*   *   *   *   *

J.G.Kohl's account has been sub-divided for the convenience of local and family historians.

Travels in Ireland – Part 1, takes us through Edgeworthtown, The Shannon, Limerick, Edenvale, Kilrush and Father Mathew.

Travels in Ireland – Part 2, his journey continues through Tarbet, Tralee, Killarney, Bantry, Cork, Kilkenny and Waterford.

Travels in Ireland – Part 3, this section deals with Wexford, Enniscorthy, Avoca, Glendalough and Dublin.

Travels In Ireland - Part 4 – he goes north for the last part of his journey through Dundalk, Newry, Belfast, The Antrim Coast, Rathlin, The Giant's Causeway.

* *   *   *   *

Henry D. Inglis' account has also been sub-divided for the convenience of local and family historians.

A Journey throughout Ireland, During the Spring, Summer and Autumn of 1834, Part 1 takes us from Dublin. Through Wexford, Waterford and Cork.

A Journey throughout Ireland, During the Spring, Summer and Autumn of 1834, Part 2 is an account of Kerry, Clare, Limerick and the Shannon and concludes in Athlone.

*   *   *   *   *

Stephen Gwynn's account has also been sub-divided for the convenience of local and family historians.

Highways and Byways in Donegal and Antrim Part One: Donegal

Highways and Byways in Donegal and Antrim Part: Two - Derry & Co. Antrim

*   *   *   *   *

Aghaidh Achadh Mór, The Face of Aghamore – edited by Joe Byrne.
This is a reproduction of a title originally published in 1991 and is of enduring interest to local historians and to those with ancestral roots in East Mayo. It covers such topics as Stone Age archaeology, family history, local hedge schools, O'Carolan's connection with the parish, the Civil War and townland surveys.

Lough Corrib, Its Shores and Islands: with Notices of Lough Mask - by William R. Wilde, first published in 1867. In the words of the author: 'A work intended to … rescue from oblivion, or preserve from desecration, some of the historic monuments of the country'.

A Statistical and Agricultural Survey of the Co. of Galway – by Hely Dutton
Dutton's survey has resulted in a detailed description of the agricultural conditions and practices of Galway in the early Nineteenth Century. He has added detailed chronologies of the leading officials of Galway town and its governance, as well as of the senior churchmen of the bishopric of Tuam and the abbeys, monasteries and convents, of the area.

A History of Sligo: Town and Country, Vol. I, by Terrence O'Rorke
This classic and well-loved history, first published in 1889, is the work of a man born and bred in Sligo. It remains a work of fascination for anyone with connections to Sligo, and is an important reference for anyone interested in the history of Ireland.

A Step Up – by Pat Nolan
This is the story of the one of the great Irish fishing vessels, the BIM 56-footers. The book contains details on each boat, and recollections of individuals who owned and/or fished on them.

*   *   *   *   *

Poems, Ballads and Songs

Songs of the Glens of Antrim, Moiré O'Neill
These Songs of the Glens of Antrim were written by a Glenswoman in the dialect of the Glens, and chiefly for the pleasure of other Glens-people.

Clachan
Publishing

Clachan Publishing, Ballycastle, Glens of Antrim.